Living in
NORTHERN IRELAND

Annabelle Lynch

W
FRANKLIN WATTS
LONDON • SYDNEY

First published in 2014 by
Franklin Watts
338 Euston Road
London
NW1 3BH

Franklin Watts Australia
Level 17/207 Kent Street
Sydney
NSW 2000

HB ISBN 978 1 4451 2796 5
Library ebook ISBN 978 1 4451 2800 9

Dewey number: 941.6'083
A CIP catalogue record for this book is
available from the British Library.

Series Editor: Julia Bird
Series Design: D.R. ink

Printed in China

Franklin Watts is a division of
Hachette Children's Books,
an Hachette UK company.
www.hachette.co.uk

Contents

Welcome to Northern Ireland! 4

People in Northern Ireland 6

Cities 8

Countryside and waterways 10

The Giant's Causeway 12

What we eat 14

Having fun 16

Famous places 18

Festivals and celebrations 20

Northern Ireland: Fast facts 22

Glossary 23

Index 24

Words in bold are in the glossary on page 23.

Welcome to Northern Ireland!

Welcome to Northern Ireland! Northern Ireland is one of the four countries of the United Kingdom.

Northern Ireland in the UK

Northern Ireland is part of the island of Ireland, but only Northern Ireland is part of the UK. The rest of Ireland is known as the Republic of Ireland. The Irish Sea lies between Northern Ireland and the rest of the UK.

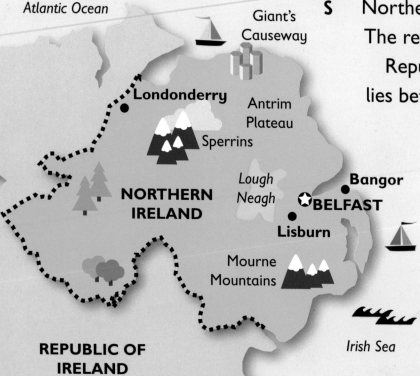

Atlantic Ocean

Giant's Causeway

Londonderry

Antrim Plateau

Sperrins

NORTHERN IRELAND

Lough Neagh

Bangor

BELFAST

Lisburn

Mourne Mountains

REPUBLIC OF IRELAND

Irish Sea

SCOTLAND

NORTHERN IRELAND

ENGLAND

WALES

Up and down

There are two big mountain **ranges** in Northern Ireland – the Sperrins and the Mourne Mountains. The rest of the land is rolling green hills with lots of rivers and **valleys**.

The Mourne Mountains are the highest mountains in Northern Ireland.

Weather

The weather in Northern Ireland changes every day! Usually the **climate** is mild and wet with warm summers and cool winters.

People in Northern Ireland

Hello! I come from Northern Ireland. People from Northern Ireland are called Northern Irish.

Around 1.8 million people live in Northern Ireland. It has the smallest **population** of all of the countries in the United Kingdom.

Where people live

Lots of people live close to the **capital** city of Belfast, where they can find work. Fewer people live on the coast or in the mountains.

Belfast is located on the coast of Northern Ireland.

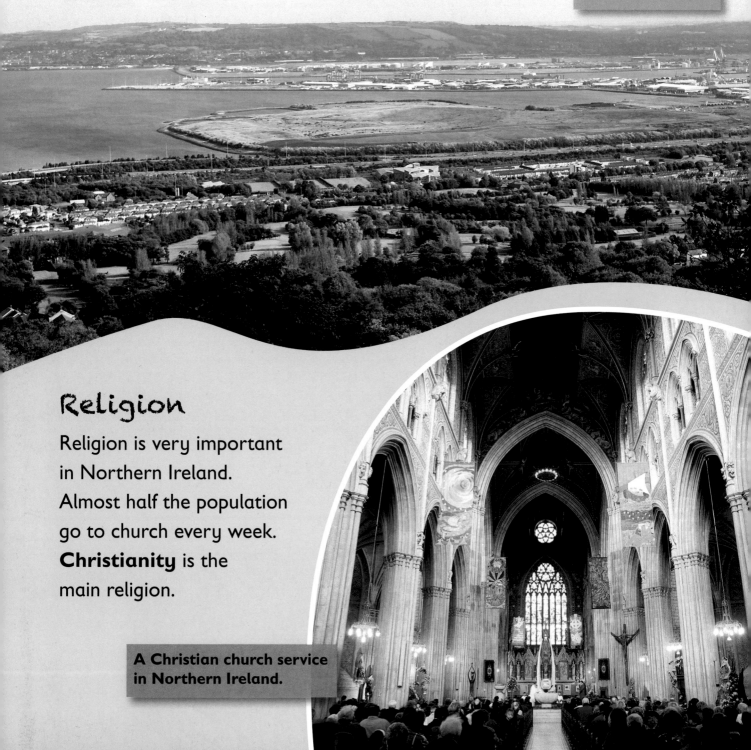

Religion

Religion is very important in Northern Ireland. Almost half the population go to church every week. **Christianity** is the main religion.

A Christian church service in Northern Ireland.

Cities

I live in Belfast. Belfast is the biggest city in Northern Ireland. Around 580,000 people live in or around Belfast.

World of work

Lots of people come to Belfast to work. In the past, shipbuilding was one of the main **industries** here. Today, people work in lots of different industries. Many people work for the **government**, which is based in Belfast.

Belfast City Hall is in the centre of Belfast.

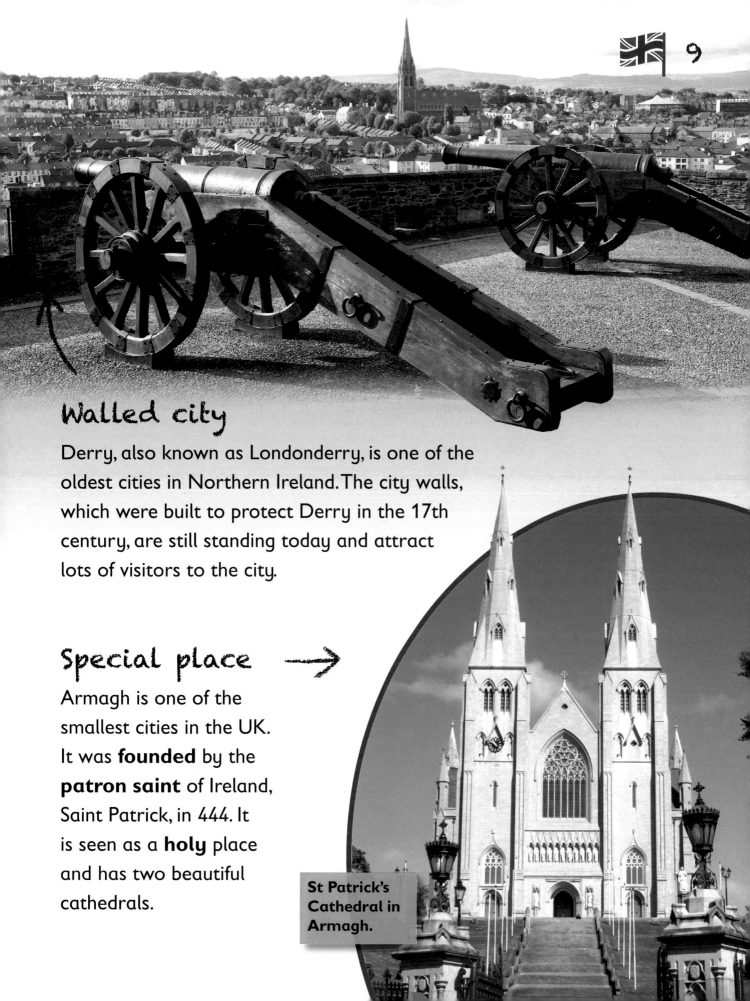

Walled city

Derry, also known as Londonderry, is one of the oldest cities in Northern Ireland. The city walls, which were built to protect Derry in the 17th century, are still standing today and attract lots of visitors to the city.

Special place →

Armagh is one of the smallest cities in the UK. It was **founded** by the **patron saint** of Ireland, Saint Patrick, in 444. It is seen as a **holy** place and has two beautiful cathedrals.

St Patrick's Cathedral in Armagh.

Countryside and waterways

I live in the countryside of Northern Ireland. It is very green and beautiful!

Farming

The countryside is great for farming. Apples, plums and cherries grow in the **orchards**, and potatoes are farmed across the land. Sheep and cows graze in the fields.

Large lake

Lough Neagh is found in the heart of Northern Ireland. It is the biggest lake in the UK and supplies almost half of Northern Ireland's water.

Wildlife

Lough Neagh is a great place to go birdwatching. Northern Ireland is home to many **rare** birds, such as red kites and peregrine falcons. The coast is also full of wildlife. Seals, dolphins and even sharks can be spotted swimming in the Irish Sea.

Old story

Legend says that long ago a giant called Finn McCool threw a huge handful of rocks at another giant. The rocks fell in the sea, forming the Isle of Man. The hole where the rocks had once been filled with water to become Lough Neagh.

Red kite

The Giant's Causeway

The Giant's Causeway in Northern Ireland is one of the most famous places in the world. If you are in Northern Ireland, you must visit it!

Cool rocks

The Giant's Causeway is an amazing rocky landscape on the coast of Northern Ireland. It is made up of around 40,000 columns of dark rock. Some of the columns have six sides, but others have seven or even eight sides.

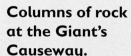

Columns of rock at the Giant's Causeway.

How it formed

The Giant's Causeway was formed over 60 million years when **volcanic eruptions** led to hot rock suddenly spilling out across the coastline. As it cooled, the rock formed into a pattern of columns which fitted together. Some are over 10 metres high.

Popular place

Today, the Giant's Causeway is Northern Ireland's most popular **tourist** attraction. Millions of people come to explore this strange landscape for themselves.

Dry feet

Some people say that Finn McCool made the Giant's Causeway so he could cross the sea to Scotland without getting his boots wet!

What we eat

We eat lots of different foods in Northern Ireland. Some foods are the same as in other countries of the UK. Others are special to Northern Ireland.

Ulster fry

For breakfast, we might have an Ulster fry. This is fried or grilled bacon, sausage and egg, served with crispy Irish potato or **soda bread**. We might add **black pudding**, baked beans, mushrooms and tomatoes, too.

← Irish stew

Almost everyone enjoys a traditional Irish stew. This is made with lamb or beef, potato, onion and carrot and flavoured with lots of pepper. It is often eaten with buttery bread. Delicious!

Snacks

Yellow man is a traditional Irish sweet snack. It tastes a bit like honeycomb. We also like eating dulse, which is crunchy, salted seaweed – fresh from the sea!

Famous drink

Ireland is most famous for making a drink called Guinness. It is sold all over the world.

Having fun

We love to have fun in Northern Ireland! There is lots to do outdoors. We also love playing and watching sport.

On your bike

It is always good fun to get out and about on our bikes. Northern Ireland has some great biking trails to tackle. They are graded so you know how hard or easy they are before you set off!

The beach at Cushendun.

By the sea

Northern Ireland has some fantastic sandy beaches. When the weather is sunny, we go to the coast to swim, sail, surf or just explore.

Sport

Golf is very popular here and some Northern Irish players, such as Rory McIlroy, are among the world's best. We also like playing and watching football and rugby, as well as some traditional Irish sports such as **hurling**.

Famous places

Northern Ireland has lots of exciting places to visit, both in the city and in the countryside.

The Titanic Visitor Centre in Belfast.

Sinking ship

Titanic Belfast is Belfast's top attraction. Visit it to find out all about the story of the famous ship *Titanic*, which was built in a Belfast shipyard. It sank in 1912 after hitting an iceberg in the Atlantic Ocean.

ÉIRE £1

TITANIC

1999

Old castle

Carrickfergus Castle was built in the 12th century and used by the army up until 1928. Today you can explore it for yourself and find out all about its long history.

Did you know?

Lots of TV shows are filmed in Northern Ireland, including CBBC's 'Dani's Castle'.

Up in the air

If you are feeling brave, walk across the rope bridge to Carrick-a-Rede island! The bridge hangs 30 wobbly metres above the sea and only eight people can walk across it at a time.

Festivals and celebrations

We celebrate lots of the same festivals in Northern Ireland as in the rest of UK, such as Christmas and Divali. Some are special to Northern Ireland, though.

Fun for kids

The Children's Festival takes place in Belfast in March every year. There is music, art, Irish dance and storytelling. Everybody can join in!

Irish dancing.

Saint Patrick's Day celebrations.

Famous day

Saint Patrick is the patron saint of Ireland. On 17 March every year, we celebrate Saint Patrick's Day. There are street **parades** and parties. We sing songs, wave flags, and wear shamrocks and funny hats. It's great fun!

Lucky leaf

The green shamrock is a **symbol** for Ireland. It is meant to bring good luck.

Northern Ireland: Fast facts

Capital: Belfast

Population: 1.81 million (2011)

Area: 13,843 square km

Languages: English, Irish

Currency: Pound sterling

Main religions: Christianity

Longest river: River Bann (129 km)

Highest mountain: Slieve Donard (850 m)

National holidays: New Year's Day (1 January), St Patrick's Day (17 March), Good Friday, Easter Sunday, first Monday in May, last Monday in May, Orangemen's Day (on or near 12 July), last Monday in August, Christmas Day (25 December), Boxing Day (26 December)

Glossary

black pudding a dark sausage made of pork and pig's blood

capital the city in which the government of a country meets

Christianity a religion based around the words of Jesus Christ

climate the usual weather in a place

founded to set up or begin

government the group of people who run a country

holy special to a religion

hurling a game played by two teams with sticks and balls

industry type of work

legend an old story

orchard a garden of fruit trees

parade when a group of people walk or drive slowly through a place. Parades usually celebrate a special occasion

patron saint a holy person who is believed to look after a particular country or place

population the number of people living in a place

range a group

rare not usual or common

soda bread a type of bread made with sodium bicarbonate instead of yeast

symbol something that stands for something else

tourist someone who visits a place on holiday

valley a low area of land between two hills

volcanic eruption when hot rocks and ashes are thrown out of a volcano

Index

A
Armagh 9

B
Belfast 4, 7, 8, 18, 20, 22

C
Carrick-a-Rede 19
Carrickfergus Castle 19
celebrations 20–21
Children's Festival 20
Christianity 7, 9, 22
cities 4, 7, 8–9, 18
coast 7, 11, 12–13, 17
countryside 5, 7, 10–11,
    16–18
cycling 16

F
farming 10
festivals 20–21
food 14–15

G
Giant's Causeway 4, 12–13
golf 17

H
holidays, national 22
hurling 17

I
Irish dance 20

L
Londonderry 4, 9
Lough Neagh 4, 11

M
McCool, Finn 11, 13
mountains 4, 5, 7, 22
Mourne Mountains 4, 5
music 20

P
people 6–7
population 6, 22

R
religion 7, 9, 21, 22

S
Saint Patrick 9, 21
Saint Patrick's Day 21, 22
shamrock 21
Sperrins 4, 5
sport 16–17

T
Titanic Belfast 18
tourism 9, 13, 18, 19

W
weather 5
wildlife 11
work 7, 8